Fort Lauderdale Memories

A Postcard History
1900-1960

Todd L. Bothel

Schiffer Publishing Ltd®

4880 Lower Valley Road, Atglen Pennsylvania 19310

Other Schiffer Books on Related Subjects:

Greetings from Daytona Beach,
978-0-7643-2806-0, $24.95

Greetings from Ormond Beach,
978-0-7643-2809-1, $24.95

St. Petersburg: Past and Present,
978-0-7643-2903-6, $24.95

Designed by Stephanie Daugherty
Type set in Goudy/Souvenir Lt BT
ISBN: 978-0-7643-2828-2
Printed in China

Schiffer Books are available at special discounts for bulk purchases for sales promotions or premiums. Special editions, including personalized covers, corporate imprints, and excerpts can be created in large quantities for special needs. For more information contact the publisher:

Published by Schiffer Publishing Ltd.
4880 Lower Valley Road
Atglen, PA 19310
Phone: (610) 593-1777; Fax: (610) 593-2002
E-mail: Info@schifferbooks.com

For the largest selection of fine reference books on this and related subjects, please visit our web site at **www.schifferbooks.com.**
We are always looking for people to write books on new and related subjects. If you have an idea for a book please contact us at the above address.

This book may be purchased from the publisher. Include $5.00 for shipping. Please try your bookstore first. You may write for a free catalog.

In Europe, Schiffer books are distributed by
Bushwood Books
6 Marksbury Ave.
Kew Gardens
Surrey TW9 4JF England
Phone: 44 (0) 20 8392-8585; Fax: 44 (0) 20 8392-9876
E-mail: info@bushwoodbooks.co.uk
Website: www.bushwoodbooks.co.uk
Free postage in the U.K., Europe; air mail at cost.

Dedication

This book is dedicated to my father, Curt Bothel, who always provided support for my endeavors and encouraged me to make my own decisions.

Acknowledgements

The Fort Lauderdale Historical Society was founded in 1962 to collect and preserve the history of Fort Lauderdale, Florida. The Society maintains and operates five historic buildings in downtown Fort Lauderdale. All of the postcards featured in this book come from the Society's large archival collection located in the Hoch Heritage Center. The "P" number associated with each postcard (and that appear at the end of the captions) is the Historical Society's postcard catalog number.

Contents

Chapter One:

In the Beginning:
An Overview of Fort Lauderdale

From its humble beginnings as a United States Army outpost during the Second Seminole War, Fort Lauderdale has grown from a produce shipping point to a five-star resort town in little less than one hundred years. The New River Settlement began in the 1780s with Surles and Frankee Lewis as the first family to establish a farm, ten miles inland on the river. By 1830 there were fifty residents in the area including the William Cooley family.

The Second Seminole War broke out on December 28, 1835 with the Dade Massacre near Tampa. On January 6, 1836 a group of Seminoles attacked and killed the Cooley family. In response Major General Thomas Jesup eventually sent Major William Lauderdale and two hundred mounted Tennessee Volunteers to establish a fort on the New River in March of 1838. After one minor skirmish with the Seminoles, the base was abandoned that May. A second temporary fort was built in February 1839 at Tarpon Bend until a permanent "Fort Lauderdale" was built at the beach. The fort was occupied until the end of the war in 1842.

Through the rest of the nineteenth century, apart from some Seminole camps, there were few inhabitants in the area, besides farmer John "Pig" Brown and the keepers at House of Refuge Number 4. In 1892 a road between Lantana and Lemon City (North Miami) was completed and the Biscayne Bay Stage Line opened an overnight camp at the ferry crossing on New River. In 1893 stage line manager Guy Metcalf hired his cousin Frank Stranahan to manage the ferry and camp.

Following the Great Freeze of 1894-1895 in northern Florida, people started moving into the area; setting up farms, they would send their produce and citrus north by boat. In 1896 Henry Flagler's Florida East Coast Railway established a station at Fort Lauderdale and this allowed for greater and quicker exchange of supplies and people. With the start of the Everglades Drainage Project in 1906, anticipation of more farmland enticed many people from the north to come to Fort Lauderdale. In 1911 Richard Bolles held his land lottery and 3,000 new residents poured into the small village. This influx spurred the original 143 inhabitants to incorporate the Town of Fort Lauderdale to deal with the need for municipal services and control over development.

Growth continued through the teens and early 1920s as Fort Lauderdale became a major agricultural shipping point and land speculators and tin can tourists arrived from the north. The development of new land tracts and the reconfiguration of the natural environment changed the fortunes of many

"Greetings from Fort Lauderdale." (P2270)

individuals and the city. Boom times persisted until the Great 1926 Hurricane created physical and economic havoc, plunging the region into the Great Depression three years ahead of the rest of the country.

Through the 1930s the area was a little sleepy winter tourist haven, but around 1937 the economy began to revive and new hotels and businesses began to open. This included the construction of the Lauderdale Beach Hotel, the first luxury hotel located on the beach. During World War II the town served as a naval aviator training center and following the war, many of these former trainees moved back to the city.

The 1950s witnessed tremendous growth in the region. Gill Construction began building affordable housing throughout the city and later transitioned to hotel construction. New hotels such as the Jolly Roger, Yankee Clipper, Tradewinds, and Lago Mar opened at the beach and began the transformation of Fort Lauderdale into a world-class tourist destination.

The 1960s opened with the release of "Where the Boys Are," which showed Fort Lauderdale in all its spring break glory. For the next thirty years the annual influx of college students brought hordes of students, which peaked at 350,000 in 1985. The 1960s also saw the arrival of Mantle and Maris, and then later Jackson, Mattingly, and Jeter as the New York Yankees arrived every year, for thirty-four years, for spring training.

Like every town in America, Fort Lauderdale has it own unique history and these postcards tell the story of its places, people and events.

Early 1900s "Greetings" with applied gold lettering. (P370)

Looking west across the New River Sound from the South Beach area. (P1192)

A 1913 Dutch Kid Pennant Message Card. (P2001)

8

DIXIE HIGHWAY, ENTRANCE TO FORT LAUDERDALE, FLORIDA.

By 1915 the local section of the Dixie Highway was complete, connecting Fort Lauderdale to the north and allowing land speculators and "tin can tourists" to drive to the region. (P2044)

The largest Banyan Tree in the United States, as purported by city promoter Commodore A. H. Brook, was once located along U.S. Highway 1. It was estimated that it would cost $2 million to move it to Vizcaya, the Deering Estate in Miami. (P1724)

2 Million Dollar Banyan Tree, Fort Lauderdale, Florida   F44

Frank Stranahan

Stranahan's Residence on New River. Ft. Lauderdale, Fla.

Phipps

Phipps

STRANAHAN & CO. FT. LAUDERDALE, FLA.

HARDWARE PAINTS
STRANAHAN & CO. DRY GOODS NOTIONS
FURNITURE
RESTAURANT.

Known as the "Father of Fort Lauderdale," Frank Stranahan arrived in 1893 to operate the New River ferry and overnight camp. He later established a trading post providing supplies to residents and trading with the Seminoles. At his trading post he started the first bank, and managed a post office and hotel. In 1901, he and his new wife, Ivy Cromartie (the town's first school teacher), had a cracker-style home (P425) built by Edwin King on the banks of the New River. By 1906 Frank had moved his store (P994) to downtown Fort Lauderdale where he ran it until 1912. The Florida East Coast Railway Bridge is in the foreground and the Wheeler Building is on the right.

10

D33:-A SEMINOLE FAMILY AT DINNER IN THE FLORIDA EVERGLADES.

PHOTO BY CHAS. C. EBBETS

(P459)⁴⁵¹⁸³

Arriving in the late eighteenth century, the Seminoles of Broward County lived in the Everglades near the Pine Island complex located about ten miles west of Fort Lauderdale. Here they lived in chickees (P459) and hunted and fished using dugout canoes (P468, P471).

Shirttail Charlie was a recognizable figure in 1920s Fort Lauderdale. According to folklore, he was sentenced to wear a dress for murdering his wife; however, it was just a traditional Seminole "big shirt." (P3049)

Scene in the Everglades, Seminole Indian in Dug-Out Canoe, Florida.

P468

Florida Seminole Indians and their Dug-Out Canoe

(P471).

12

Home of the Seminoles, near Ft. Lauderdale, Fla.

The Seminoles established a camp on West Broward Boulevard near the north fork of the New River as the photograph (P477) by Guy Phipps shows. In 1924, under the guidance of Ivy Cromartie Stranahan and Annie Jumper Tommie, the tribe moved to the Dania (Hollywood) Reservation. Both places were popular tourist attractions.

A 1902 image of the Annie Tommie Seminole Camp located at Broward Boulevard and the New River. (P2760)

Indian Camp on New River, Fort Lauderdale, Fla.

SEMINOLE INDIAN SQUAW AND FAMILY, FORT LAUDERDALE, FLORIDA

(P2031).

Shown is Panther clan matriarch Annie Jumper Tommie. Her son, Tony, was the first Seminole to attend public school in Fort Lauderdale. (P489)

ANNIE CHIEF TONYS MOTHER FT LAUDERDALE FLA

Chapter Two:

Early Life

Claiming the Everglades

In 1911 Richard Bolles conducted a lottery of soon-to-be drained Everglades land. Three thousand perspective buyers flooded into the area and established many tent cities like this one in Progresso (north Fort Lauderdale). (P2687)

With the possibility of millions of acres of new farmland being created by draining the Everglades, thousands flocked to Fort Lauderdale to purchase land. Under Richard Bolles lottery system, purchasing a lot in Progresso entitled you to a section of swampland. The influx of new residents caused the incorporation of Fort Lauderdale in 1911 in order to control development and provide municipal services.

(P519)

The Everglades Drainage Project began in 1906 with the goal of connecting the east coast of Florida with Lake Okeechobee. The North Canal was the first canal dredged. (P521)

(P524)

Early Farming

With large tracts of land becoming available with the drainage of the Everglades, farming was the major industry in the Fort Lauderdale area in the early 1900s. The rich muck soil was very conducive to growing vegetables and citrus including large cabbages (P83), strawberries (P2), and oranges (P1524).

18

The *Mason S. Moreno* brings crates of tomatoes to the shipping dock. (P2753)

Shipping Tomatoes, Ft. Lauderdale, Florida.

From the railroad yard, local produce could be sent to northern markets. The "Gateway to the Everglades" became a key vegetable shipping capital. (P2695)

Shipping Docks and R. R. Yards, Ft. Lauderdale, Fla.

Farmers offloading their tomatoes at the railroad shipping docks. (P93)

Shipping Tomatoes, Ft. Lauderdale, Florida.

View of New River, Fort Lauderdale, Florida.
Big Shipping Point for Tomatoes.

Access to the river and the newly formed canals enabled farmers to bring their produce from outlying areas to Fort Lauderdale for shipment to the north. (P2754)

Chapter Three:
A City Emerges
Early Downtown

The New River Inn was built in 1905 by Edwin King for Philemon Bryan and operated as a hotel until 1955. Today it is on the National Register of Historic Places and houses the Fort Lauderdale Museum of History. (P412)

A pre-1912 view of Brickell Avenue looking south towards the New River. The Lyric Theatre is on the left. (P3079)

Edwin King was an all-purpose builder of houses, schools, buildings, and boats. His boat works was located on the south bank of the New River. (P90)

Mr. John Kelley and W. O. Berryhill in an ox cart in front of the Everglades Grocery store on Brickell Avenue. (P2493)

Hotel Osceola, Fort Lauderdale, Fla.

BERRYHILL & CROMARTIE CO HARDWARE FARM TOOLS

In 1910, a former packing warehouse was converted into the fifty-room Hotel Osceola. (P398)

The Berryhill-Cromartie (Grocery) Store opened in 1910. (P87)

Growth of Downtown

F.L.10.   AIRPLANE VIEW OF FORT LAUDERDALE, FLA. NEW RIVER IN CENTER.

116068

**An aerial view of the downtown looking southeast towards Port Everglades
during the period of 1927-1936.** (P1797)

A 1915 view from the water tower (SW 2nd Street/Andrews Avenue) looking southeast toward Las Olas Boulevard. (P2741)

The Wanderer, a houseboat owned by famous actor Joe Jefferson, was, purportedly, Fort Lauderdale's first "party boat." (P41)

Riverside is a subdivision located between the forks of the New River. These houses were built circa 1915. (P2411)

DIXIE HIGHWAY BRIDGE OVER NEW RIVER, FORT LAUDERDALE, FLORIDA.

A 1919 view of the Andrews Avenue Bridge with *The Everglades* docked on the south bank of the New River. (P1163)

The Fort Lauderdale Women's Club was founded in 1911 to perform civic improvements. The clubhouse was built in 1917 on land donated by Frank and Ivy Stranahan at the southeast corner of Broward Boulevard and Andrews Avenue. (P1961)

The Brickell Hotel originally opened as the Hotel Gilbert in 1913. It was located in the Wheeler Building on SW 1st Avenue. The hotel closed in 1959. (P2391)

DF-74—Aerial View of Ft. Lauderdale
Port Everglades in the Background

**Aerial view of the downtown looking South towards Port Everglades.
The Governors' Club Hotel and the Broward County Courthouse are located near the center of the
image.** (P298)

A 1920s view of Andrews Avenue; looking north from New River Drive the Broward Hotel and Fort Lauderdale Hardware Store can be seen. (P2523)

Andrews Avenue looking north with the Sweet Building (left) and the Broward Hotel (right). (P1170)

At the Broward Hotel landing "one can hire boats and guides for deep sea and river fishing." The Napoleon B. Broward Drainage District Office building is on left. (P407)

DF-13—Looking North on Andrews Ave., Fort Lauderdale, Florida

The Broward Hotel (right) was demolished in 1974. Today, this view is covered by the approach to the Andrews Avenue Bridge. (P1965)

SWEET BUILDING, FORT LAUDERDALE, FLORIDA   C413

The Sweet Building was Fort Lauderdale's first skyscraper. Constructed in 1925 it opened shortly before the 1926 Hurricane. (P1999)

(P136)

FIRST FEDERAL SAVINGS AND LOAN ASSOCIATION FORT LAUDERDALE FLORIDA

Started in 1933 in the Sweet Building, the First Federal Savings and Loan moved to new offices at SE 1st Avenue and 2nd Street in 1939 (P136). **By 1947, larger facilities were needed and they constructed a new building** (P2269) **at 301 East Las Olas Boulevard.**

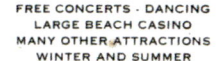

MAKE YOUR HOME IN FORT LAUDERDALE
TROPICAL WONDERLAND OF FLORIDA

REAL GULF STREAM FISHING
FINE BATHING BEACH
BOATING · GOLF · TENNIS
WINTER AND SUMMER

FREE CONCERTS · DANCING
LARGE BEACH CASINO
MANY OTHER ATTRACTIONS
WINTER AND SUMMER

NIGHT TIME ON NEW RIVER

A MID-WINTER DAY ON THE BEACH

OUR FT. LAUDERDALE OFFICE
Is the Headquarters for Sales or Rentals of
Every Type of Real Estate In and About Ft. Lauderdale

KELCY PHOTO

R. T. HODGES
207 S. ANDREWS AVE.

FORT LAUDERDALE
FLORIDA

R. T. Hodges founded his real estate business in 1924 with offices located in the Hotel Maryland building on Andrews Avenue. It was said he could show houses "by land, sea or air." (P2057)

A 1940s view of the west side of Andrews Avenue, Fort Lauderdale's main street. The McCrory's building still exists. (P1966)

In the 1930s the Hotel Maryland, McCrory's, and the First National Bank building were part of the Andrews Avenue Shopping District. (P1168)

Looking south on Andrews Avenue at the Maxwell
Arcade building prior to the 1926 Hurricane. The
Mediterranean Revival style arcade was erected
in 1925 as a retail venue. Today, it houses the
Downtowner Saloon restaurant. (P304)

A 1930s aerial view of the downtown
shows the Andrews Avenue and Florida
East Coast Railway bridges. (P294)

F. L. 108   FORT LAUDERDALE BUSINESS SECTION FROM AN AIR LINER

PHOTO BY BURWELL   4A-H1838

Air View of Fort Lauderdale, Fort Lauderdale, Florida.   *F-108*   (Hyde Photo)

A 1940s aerial view of the downtown looking northwest from SE 3rd Avenue. (P295)

34

The Main Post Office opened in 1937 with twenty-two employees at the corner of SE 1st Avenue and SE 2nd Street. (P1374)

DF.65—U. S. Post Office and Governors Club Hotel Ft. Lauderdale, Florida

U. S. Post Office, Fort Lauderdale, Florida   F-117

Built for $97,000 by the Works Progress Administration, the United States Post Office building was in service until 1974. (P2211)

F.L.8.   WILL-MAR HOTEL, FORT LAUDERDALE, FLA.

110327

The Governors' Club Hotel, Fort Lauderdale, Florida

Fort Lauderdale's first mayor, William Marshall, began construction of a new hotel downtown in 1926. When the land boom collapsed following the 1926 Hurricane, the skeleton of the building sat empty for over ten years. At left is an artist's conception of the building (P2827). In 1937, former Governor of Puerto Rico Robert Hayes Gore, and owner of the *Fort Lauderdale News*, bought the structure and opened the Governors' Club Hotel (P2281).

F.L.3. BRYAN COURT, FORT LAUDERDALE, FLA.

Tom Bryan was a second-generation businessman who established the Fort Lauderdale Light and Ice Company. He also brought telephone service to the town. Bryan Court was one of many retail and office buildings that he owned. (P2452)

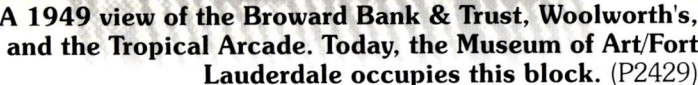

Andrews Avenue at E. Las Olas Boulevard, Ft. Lauderdale, Florida. F-65

A 1949 view of the Broward Bank & Trust, Woolworth's, and the Tropical Arcade. Today, the Museum of Art/Fort Lauderdale occupies this block. (P2429)

The Trade Winds Restaurant was located at 201 SE 1st Avenue and was open from the late 1930s to the late 1940s. (P2264)

A wintertime visitor's leisure activity was shuffleboard played at Stranahan Park. Today the Broward County Main Library is located at the site. (P2042)

FL-6   SHUFFLEBOARD PLAYERS IN STRANAHAN PARK, FORT LAUDERDALE, FLA.

6A-H1414

A view of the Andrews Avenue Shopping District in the 1940s. (P2713)

This 1950s view of the main street shopping district shows the new Burdines Building (with flag) in the background. (P1476)

Schools/Churches

A class of students at the second schoolhouse. (P125)

The town's second schoolhouse was built in 1911 of concrete block by Edwin King. This two-story building served as a school until 1915 when it became the courthouse for the newly formed Broward County. (P3081)

The Central School opened in 1915 and was located between Broward Boulevard and SE 2nd Street east of Third Avenue. Miami architect August Geiger designed the Mediterranean style building. It was demolished in 1970. (P126)

PINE CREST SCHOOL

FORT LAUDERDALE, FLORIDA   8A-H2859

In 1939, Mae McMillan opened the Pine Crest School with one hundred students in the former Edwards-Maxwell Hospital building at 1515 East Broward Boulevard. The school remained on this campus until 1965 when a new campus was built in northeast Fort Lauderdale. (P2509)

The Methodist Church was located at the site of the current Main Library and was built of concrete block by Edwin King in 1913. (P1110)

In 1920 the Presbyterian Church was erected in the 200 block of East Las Olas Boulevard. This building later served as the Chamber of Commerce building and offices for Gill Construction. (P1113)

St. Anthony's was the first Catholic church in Fort Lauderdale. The original church opened on Las Olas Boulevard in 1921. This second sanctuary, located at NE 3rd Street and NE 9th Avenue, was dedicated in 1949. (P2421)

Chapter Four

Paying Tribute
Disasters

On June 2, 1912, a fire swept through and destroyed the downtown business section of Brickell Avenue. After the fire, the town voted to form a fire department. (P285)

Escaping the 1912 fire, the Osceola Hotel burned to the ground one year later on July 17, 1913 despite the efforts of the new fire department. (P284)

During the evening of September 17 and
the early morning of September 18, 1926 a
Category 4 hurricane with a thirteen-foot storm
surge hit Fort Lauderdale head on. Almost
every structure in town suffered damage and
fifteen people lost their lives. Boats, houses,
and anything not tied down were strewn
all over town. Right, damage to the Vernon
Apartment House (P1249) at 1521 SE 2nd Court
can be seen. The large electric light sign at the
Maxwell Arcade (P1209) on Andrews Avenue
was destroyed. The hurricane signaled the end
of boom times in south Florida and started
the Great Depression in the region three years
before the rest of the country.

(P1249)

(P1209)

Patriotic

This U.S. Coast Guard parade is shown heading north on Andrews Avenue during the late 1920s or early 1930s. A Coast Guard base was located at the beach. (P312)

"The Nation's Most Beautiful Service Men's Center." Located in the former Pioneer Department Store building on East Las Olas Boulevard, it served nearly 3,000 at the weekly Saturday night dances during World War II. (P2462)

Patriotic parade headed south on Andrews Avenue in 1920. (P97)

This May 6, 1917 dated postcard shows Fort Lauderdale's first batch of World War I recruits. Photo taken at Fort Screven, Georgia. (P1186)

Chapter Five:

Growth of a City
Las Olas Boulevard

Beautiful Palm Lined Las Olas Boulevard, by moonlight, Fort Lauderdale, Florida   F-112

Las Olas Boulevard was the first road (1917) from downtown to the beach. (P1471)

La Fiesta Room
Cocktails - Dining

BOULEVARD HOTEL
FORT LAUDERDALE
Florida

BOULEVARD HOTEL

COLONY THEATRE

Located at 448 East Las Olas Boulevard, the Boulevard Hotel operated from 1939 to 1972. Today the Huizenga Holdings Building stands on the site. (P2384)

Las Olas Boulevard,
Fort Lauderdale, Fla.

F.113

In 1927 Las Olas was dedicated to the soldiers of World War I as Memorial Boulevard. (P1175)

LAS OLAS BLVD., LOOKING TOWARD ANDREWS AVENUE, SHOWING GOVERNORS' CLUB HOTEL AND SWEET BUILDING. FORT LAUDERDALE, FLORIDA
C412

The Governors Club HOTEL

In the late 1940s and 1950s the Las Olas Boulevard shopping district expanded and started the shift of the retail center out of downtown. (P1745)

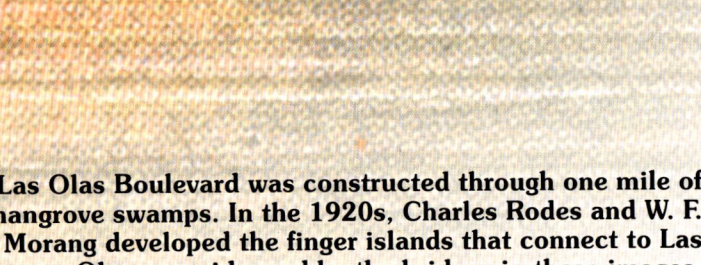

D. F. 6—Famous Royal Palms along Las Olas Blvd., Fort Lauderdale, Fla.

1B-H911

(P1742)

Las Olas Boulevard, Fort Lauderdale, Florida

F-140

(P2437)

Las Olas Boulevard was constructed through one mile of mangrove swamps. In the 1920s, Charles Rodes and W. F. Morang developed the finger islands that connect to Las Olas, as evidenced by the bridges in these images.

Houses

The Las Olas finger islands generated semi-secluded waterfront property on which some very nice residences have been built.

DF-15 Hendricks Island in the City of South Sea Islands Fort Lauderdale, Florida

(P1396)

DF.71—Las Olas Blvd. and Island Homes Ft. Lauderdale, Florida

(P1739)

D. F. 28—"Pretty Florida Bungalows" in Fort Lauderdale

D313:-A BEAUTIFUL HOME. FORT LAUDERDALE. FLORIDA

Pretty Florida Bungalows in Fort Lauderdale. (P2460)

Written on the back of the card: "Fort Lauderdale is a city of beautiful homes. Residents from northern states have established magnificent residences along the banks of the New River." (P1386)

AT THE ERKINS HOME, FORT LAUDERDALE, FLORIDA

Casa Sonriendo was the 1920s era, Francis Abreu designed home of A. W. Erkins. (P433)

Through the 1950s, Fort Lauderdale experienced a 139% increase in population; the Quinn Home at 501 Riviera Isle (P450) **and other island homes, according to Dottie Wilcox, made Fort Lauderdale "the place to retire to—none better."** (P1700)

DF-43—Beautiful Island Home, Fort Lauderdale, Fla.

(P1700)

DF-40—"The Venice of America," Fort Lauderdale, Fla.

(P450)

One of the many island waterfront homes. (P1699)

DF-11—An Island Waterfront Home, Fort Lauderdale, Florida

Gateway Shopping Center

Opened in 1950 on the site of the former Clyde Beatty Zoo, the Gateway Center was Fort Lauderdale's first suburban shopping center. (P1362)

The 1960 world premiere of "Where The Boys Are" was held at The Gateway Theater (far right). (P1556)

DF69—Aerial View of the Gateway Section, Ft. Lauderdale, Fla.

DF-61—Gateway Business Section Ft. Lauderdale, Fla.

Chapter Six:

Waterways

New River

A 1920s aerial view of New River, looking east towards the Las Olas finger islands, shows the 6th Avenue (Federal Highway) Bridge near the left center of the image. (P297)

BIRDSEYE VIEW OF FORT LAUDERDALE, FLORIDA, SHOWING NEW RIVER — F-5

A circa 1937-1942 aerial view of Fort Lauderdale and the New River looking east from the Florida East Coast Railway Bridge. (P2511)

A State within a State at Ft. Lauderdale, Florida. — F-68

(Hyde Photo)

A small "Florida" peninsula on the South Fork of the New River just west of where the river splits. (P296)

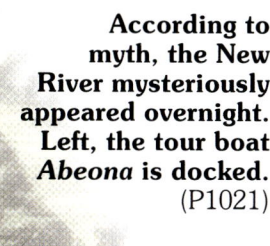

According to myth, the New River mysteriously appeared overnight. Left, the tour boat *Abeona* is docked. (P1021)

DF-20—The Fishing and Pleasure Fleet on Mysterious New River, Fort Lauderdale, Florida

F.L. 19 NEW RIVER AND BROWARD COUNTY COURT HOUSE, FORT LAUDERDALE, FLA.

This 1930s view looking west shows the 1928 Broward County Courthouse in the distance. (P2522)

A Florida Sunset
New River, Fort Lauderdale

A glorious sunset over the palm tree lined river. (P1957)

North and South New River Drives paralleled the banks of the river. A westerly view towards downtown; today New River Drive is the Riverwalk walkway. (P2468)

SOUTH NEW RIVER DRIVE, FORT LAUDERDALE, FLORIDA.

Pleasure Craft and Palms along New River, Fort Lauderdale, Florida

F19

67432

With 165 miles of navigable waterways, pleasure boats are a common sight in Fort Lauderdale. (P2274)

DF.41—Scenic New River, Fort Lauderdale, Fla.

Shown, the Federal Highway (6th Avenue) drawbridge; the Pioneer House Restaurant (Stranahan House) is to the left. The bridge was replaced in 1960 with the Henry Kinney Tunnel. (P1003)

D. F. 26 — New River at Andrews Ave. Bridge, Fort Lauderdale, Fla.

A 1940s view looking west towards downtown; the Sweet Building rises in the center of the image. (P1442)

DF-62—Moonlight on New River
Ft. Lauderdale, Fla.

DF-66—Sunset on
Mysterious New River
Ft. Lauderdale, Florida

The brilliant colors that arise during sunsets (P996) **and in the moonlight** (P995) **make the waterways of Fort Lauderdale glisten.**

Canals

F.L.9. BEVERLY HEIGHTS BY MOONLIGHT, FORT LAUDERDALE, FLA.

The Beverly Heights neighborhood is located east of Federal Highway and north of Las Olas Boulevard and is centered on the Himmarshee Canal. (P2410)

Himmarshee Canal, amidst tropical setting near Ft. Lauderdale, Florida. F-116

F-L-101 "A BEAUTIFUL PALM LINED DRIVE"

FORT LAUDERDALE, FLORIDA 3A-H612

Palms trees used to line many of Fort Lauderdale's streets and canals. (P2430)

Dredged in the 1920s, the Himmarshee Canal at one time stretched to the Federal Building at the corner of Broward Boulevard and East 3rd Avenue. Today it ends at Federal Highway (6th Avenue). (P1196)

DF-23—A Canal Scene,
Fort Lauderdale,
Florida

A lovely, secluded canal scene. (P2463)

DF-14— One of the many Canals,
Fort Lauderdale, Florida

Fort Lauderdale has an expansive and intricate canal system that includes some nice secluded spots. (P2439)

Port Everglades

AT PORT EVERGLADES FLA.
—FEB. 18TH 1935—

(P1109)

FL-115   LARGE OCEAN LINER DOCKED AT PORT EVERGLADES

BETWEEN FORT LAUDERDALE AND HOLLYWOOD, FLA.

PHOTO BY BURWELL

(P2415)

Port Everglades opened in 1928 after many attempts to establish a deepwater port. Since its inception it has served as both a cargo and cruise ship port of call. The *S.S. Columbia* of the Panama-Pacific Line (P2415) and the *Duchess of Richmond* (P1109) were visitors in the 1930s.

DF.54—Aerial View of Port Everglades
Ft. Lauderdale, Florida

The escort aircraft carrier *USS Charger* at Port Everglades following World War II. (P2416)

On December 19, 1939 the British cruiser *Orion* chased the German cargo vessel *Arauca* into Port Everglades. The vessel was interned there until the United States entry into World War II, when it was seized and retrofitted as an American vessel. (P1101)

GERMAN FREIGHTER ARAUCA
PORT EVERGLADES, FLA.

Chapter Seven

Beach Scenes
The Beach

Written on the back of the card: "This beach is a favorite with all South Florida. Gently sloping and free from undertow." (P1995)

In the early days the beach was only accessible by boat and was underused and undeveloped. (P1010)

A WINTER DAY, LAS OLAS BEACH, FORT LAUDERDALE, FLORIDA

With the opening of the Las Olas Bridge in 1917, the beach became much more accessible. (P34)

By the 1920s the beach had become a tourist destination. (P27)

FL-102   FORT LAUDERDALE MUNICIPAL BEACH ON A JANUARY DAY

PHOTO BY KELCY

3A-H670

LAS OLAS BEACH, FT. LAUDERDALE, FLORIDA

From the back of the card: The beach is "easily accessible from every section of the city." (P36)

The beach offered a variety of activities for residents and visitors alike. (P1996)

THE BEACH, FORT LAUDERDALE, FLORIDA

Bathing at Las Olas Beach, Fort Lauderdale, Fla.

Everybody enjoys the warm waters during the winter. (P2508)

68

BIRD'S-EYE VIEW ALONG THE OCEAN FRONT. BEAUTIFUL FORT LAUDERDALE. FLORIDA

E-4339

The Lauderdale Beach Hotel (center) was the first luxury hotel at the beach.
This circa 1937-1945 image shows the largely undeveloped beach area. (P2551)

During the 1920s a diving platform was located at the beach. (P2507)

Written on the back of the card: "Las Olas Beach is not excelled anywhere in the world." (P1993)

The closeness of the Gulf Stream current to the Florida coast helps keep the ocean water warm near Fort Lauderdale. (P23)

The beach in front of the Lauderdale Beach Hotel. (P2506)

DF-63—Sun, Sand and Surf on Tropical Ft. Lauderdale Beach, Fla.

F. L. 16   BATHERS AT LAS OLAS BEACH, FORT LAUDERDALE, FLA.

Another enjoyable day at the beach. (P1994)

DF-58—Colorful Ft. Lauderdale Beach Ft. Lauderdale, Fla.

During the late 1930s cabanas made their appearance at the beach along the boardwalk. (P1284)

DF.29—Colorful Beach, Fort Lauderdale, Fla.

Cabanas add color and shade to the beach. (P28)

Just Arrived in Ft. Lauderdale, Florida

DF68—North Beach and Birch Park Section
Ft. Lauderdale, Fla.   2C-H434

Following Hugh Taylor Birch's passing in 1946, his three miles of property along the beach was developed into apartment houses and hotels. He also donated a large section of land, which became Birch State Park (upper right corner). (P1299)

D. F. 32—Bathers on the Beach at Fort Lauderdale, Florida

A 1947 view of the south end of the beach. (P1535)

Besides the swimwear, little has changed during a day at the beach.
(P1309)

A colorful beach, Florida

Photo: E. Ludwig, John Hinde Studios.

Boardwalk and Beach, Sunny
Fort Lauderdale, Florida   F47

The boardwalk along the beach at Las Olas Boulevard and Florida State Road A1A.
(P2781)

Fort Lauderdale Beach and cabanas, Florida.

Photo: E. Ludwig, John Hinde Studios.

Development of the beach continued through the 1950s and 1960s, and renewal efforts continue today. This view is quite different today. (P1308)

From the back of the card: "Where The Boys Are during spring vacation is no mystery at Fort Lauderdale Beach." (P1540)

Casino Pool

Swimming Pool in Municipal Casino on the Beach at Fort Lauderdale, Florida

The Casino Pool, which opened in 1928, featured an Olympic-sized pool filled daily with ocean water. It was a Mediterranean Revival style structure. (P1302)

Designed by Francis Abreu, the pool was the site of the annual College Swim Forum that started in 1935. (P22)

THE BEACH CASINO

In 1936 two locals participated in the Olympics. Katy Rawls, winner of thirty national titles in swimming and diving, trained at the Casino Pool. Later she was one of the original twenty-eight Women's Auxiliary Ferrying Squadron (WAFS) pilots in World War II. Meanwhile, Les McNeece played second base on the American demonstration team. He hit the walk off game-winning homerun. (P2927)

In 1966, the Casino Pool was leveled to make way for the International Swimming Hall of Fame. (P1547)

Hall of Fame Pool, Fort Lauderdale.

Bahia Mar Yacht Basin

DF-50   Bahia Mar from the Ocean
Fort Lauderdale, Fla.

**Following World War II, the city bought the former Coast Guard base for $600,000
and residents supported a $2.5 million bond for construction.** (P1571)

(P414)

DF.56—Bahia Mar and Ft. Lauderdale Beach Looking North

Looking north from Mayan Lake (P1799), the triangular piece of land (lower right corner) where the Yankee Clipper Hotel (P414) was built in 1956 can be seen. Designed to look like an ocean liner, it featured an ice show and a Polynesian revue. It was owned and operated by George Gill, who developed many of the hotels at the beach.

(P1799)

DF.72—Bahia-Mar Yacht Basin
Ft. Lauderdale, Florida

DF.57—Bahia Mar Yacht Basin,
Fort Lauderdale, Fla.

Bahia Mar has allowed Fort Lauderdale to become the "Yachting Capital of the World." (P1312)

Bahia Mar annually attracts thousands of yachtsmen and is the host of the annual boat show. (P2891)

DF.45

Bahia Mar is located at the site of
the third Fort Lauderdale. The House
of Refuge Number 4 also formerly
occupied this site. (P1798)

DF-60—The Plaza at Bahia Mar
Ft. Lauderdale, Fla.

Opened in December 1949, the Bahia
Mar complex also included a post office, a
restaurant, and a shopping center. (P1565)

Chapter Eight:

Recreation

Boating

Prior to 1917, the only way to reach the beach was by boat. These residents are heading to the beach for a Sunday afternoon picnic. (P54)

In 1921 President-elect Warren Harding visited Fort Lauderdale. Here he is (third from the left) onboard Commodore Brook's sailboat *Klyo*. (P319)

Off for the Beach! July 4th 1912
Ft. Lauderdale Fla.

Guy Phipps captures the *Okeechobee* on its way to the beach for the 1912 Fourth of July celebration. (P50)

STEAMER SUWANEE, FT. LAUDERDALE, FLA. 2834
PHOTO BY PHIPPS

After the canals connected Fort Lauderdale to Lake Okeechobee and the lake to the west coast of Florida, people could embark on a two-day trip aboard the *Suwanee* to Fort Myers. (P58)

The ABEONA
docked at Andrews Bridge — Ft. Lauderdale, Fla.

The *Abeona* provided a three-hour jungle cruise for visitors down the New River with narration from Mayor Will Reed. (P1577)

At right is "Captain" Al Starts tour showboat, the *Southern Belle*. Starts began with the *Jungle Queen* in the 1930s and by the 1960s he was operating the *Southern Belle*. (P56)

A Tranquil Florida Waterway

The Water Taxi is an important part of public transportation for the city. (P1197)

Since its earliest days, boats have been an important fixture in Fort Lauderdale. (P1440)

AN EVERY-DAY SCENE AT FORT LAUDERDALE, FLORIDA.

Fishing

Sailfish, tarpon, and many other types of fish can be caught around Fort Lauderdale. (P1145)

1936-1937 Anglers' Contest results. Lots of big fish. (P2494)

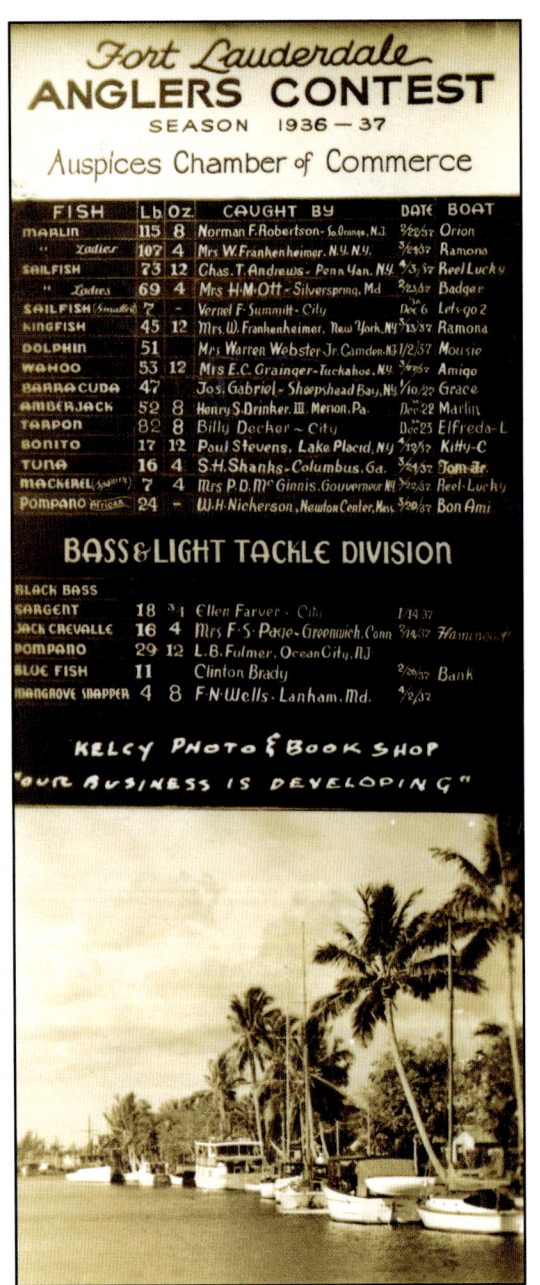

Fort Lauderdale ANGLERS CONTEST
SEASON 1936—37
Auspices Chamber of Commerce

FISH	Lb	Oz	CAUGHT BY	DATE	BOAT
MARLIN	115	8	Norman F. Robertson - So. Orange, N.J.	3/22/37	Orion
" Ladies	107	4	Mrs. W. Frankenheimer, N.Y. N.Y.	3/24/37	Ramona
SAILFISH	73	12	Chas. T. Andrews - Penn Yan. N.Y.	4/3/37	Reel Lucky
" Ladies	69	4	Mrs. H.M. Ott - Silverspring, Md.	3/23/37	Badger
SAILFISH (Smallest)	7	-	Vernel F. Summitt - City	Dec. 6	Let's go 2
KINGFISH	45	12	Mrs. W. Frankenheimer, New York, N.Y.	3/13/37	Ramona
DOLPHIN	51		Mrs. Warren Webster Jr. Camden. N.J.	1/2/37	Mousie
WAHOO	53	12	Mrs. E.C. Grainger - Tuckahoe, N.Y.	3/26/37	Amigo
BARRACUDA	47		Jos. Gabriel - Sheepshead Bay, N.Y.	1/10/37	Grace
AMBERJACK	52	8	Henry S. Drinker. III. Merion, Pa.	Dec. 22	Marlin
TARPON	82	8	Billy Decker - City	Dec. 23	Elfreda-L
BONITO	17	12	Paul Stevens, Lake Placid, N.Y.	3/19/37	Kitty-C
TUNA	16	4	S.H. Shanks - Columbus, Ga.	3/24/37	Tom Jr.
MACKEREL (Spanish)	7	4	Mrs. P.D. McGinnis. Gouverneur N.Y.	3/22/37	Reel Lucky
POMPANO (African)	24	-	W.H. Nicherson, Newton Center, Mass.	3/20/37	Bon Ami

BASS & LIGHT TACKLE DIVISION

FISH	Lb	Oz	CAUGHT BY	DATE
BLACK BASS				
SARGENT	18	1	Ellen Farver - City	1/14/37
JACK CREVALLE	16	4	Mrs. F.S. Page - Greenwich, Conn	3/14/37
POMPANO	29	12	L.B. Fulmer, Ocean City, N.J.	
BLUE FISH	11		Clinton Brady	2/26/37
MANGROVE SNAPPER	4	8	F.N. Wells - Lanham, Md.	1/2/37

KELCY PHOTO & BOOK SHOP
"OUR BUSINESS IS DEVELOPING"

Local model Dorothy Crowder, onboard the *Tia Juana*, lands a thirty-pound Sailfish during the 1946 Anglers' Contest. (P1463)

Daily catch from aboard the *Betty J II*. (P2426)

Sports

A 1940s view of the Fort Lauderdale Yacht Club located at the end of SE 12th Street. (P2706)

The West Side Golf and Country Club was built in 1926 in what is now Plantation. (P1128)

Shown is the 1914-1915 Lauderdale High School Baseball Team. (P1134)

N. Y. Yankees at Ft. Lauderdale, Fla.

To entice and convince the New York Yankees to move their spring training operations to Fort Lauderdale, the city built a new baseball stadium in 1962. Today, this same stadium is used by the Baltimore Orioles. (P1461)

Chapter Nine:

Noteable Places & Buildings
Hillsboro Lighthouse

Opened in 1907, the Hillsboro Lighthouse marks the northern limit of the Florida reef. The 147-foot tall structure was constructed by the Russell Wheel & Foundry Company of Detroit, Michigan and features a fresnel lens. In the 1990s the lighthouse underwent restoration and in 2003 was honored with a commemorative stamp from the U.S. Postal Service.

(P2063)

Sunrise at Hillsboro Lighthouse near Pompano, Florida.

(P2465)

Hillsboro Light House, Fort Lauderdale, Fla.

(P315)

Hotels/Apartments

THE MOZELLE HOTEL — 824 S. E. 2nd COURT — FT. LAUDERDALE, FLA.

A Home Away from Home, Situated in the Residential District

9B-H1629

Typed on the back of the card: "All rooms with Running Water and a Shower." (P395)

This promotional postcard for the Jones Sun Court Apartments and Motel espouses the virtues of Fort Lauderdale. (P1673)

Lauderdale the Venice of America has seven miles of public beach, hundreds of charter fishing boats, sightseeing boats and numerous lovely golf courses. Fort Lauderdale is the Most Tropical City in the U.S.A. because it is five hundred miles south of the southernmost boundary of California, and the Gulf Stream flows 1 ½ miles off the coast.

Maxwell Hotel, 441 S. Andrews Ave., Ft. Lauderdale, Florida

The Maxwell opened in 1942 and stayed open until 1986. The building still stands at the south end of the Andrews Avenue Bridge. (P2779)

HOTEL CHAMP CARR

FORT LAUDERDALE, FLORIDA

Today the Riverside Hotel, the Hotel Champ Carr opened in 1936 and was named after the manager, a local fishing boat mate. (P2467)

HOTEL BROWARD, FORT LAUDERDALE, FLA. 49.

(P408)

The Hotel Broward (P408) was Fort Lauderdale's first
tourist hotel and was located just north of the New
River on Andrews Avenue. Designed by prominent
architect August Geiger, it featured an exquisite lobby
(P2459). The first guests were the cast and crew of the
famous D. W. Griffith film company, who were in town
to shoot the movie "Idol Dancer."

The Hotel Broward was completed in 1919 after local
residents contributed $29,000 when the developer
ran out of money. It remained open until 1974. Bubier
Park/DDA Plaza is now located at the site. (P2747)

HOTEL BROWARD LOBBY, FORT LAUDERDALE, FLORIDA

(P2459)

HOTEL BROWARD, FORT LAUDERDALE'S FINEST HOSTELRY (STEAM HEATED)

(P2747)

The Tarpon Hotel opened in 1924 and remained open until 1950. In later years it was the Hotel Maryland. (P2641)

Formerly a U.S. Navy monitor that saw action during the Spanish-American War, the *Amphitrite* was converted to a floating hotel in 1919 and was brought to Fort Lauderdale in 1931. (P403)

Originally built in 1902 as a hunting lodge for John McGregor Adams by Edwin King, in 1914 D. C. Alexander purchased the Las Olas Inn and it was the first hotel opened at the beach (P2692). By the late 1940s beach development began to encroach on the property (P419) and in 1954 the building was demolished. From 1969-1992, the Oceanside Holiday Inn was located at the site.

(P2692)

(P419)

Lauderdale Beach Hotel, Fort Lauderdale, Florida

F-126

(P2517)

Built for $200,000 by the Charellan Corporation, headed by James Knight, the Lauderdale Beach Hotel opened in 1937. Designed by Art Deco architect Roy France of Miami fame, it was the first big resort on the beach and signaled a revival of the tourist industry and Fort Lauderdale's recovery from the Great Depression. Today the larger resort hotels now located at the beach have eclipsed the Lauderdale Beach Hotel and is itself being replaced (save the front and south facades) with a new condominium/hotel tower.

The Lauderdale Beach Hotel at Fort Lauderdale, Florida

F8

(P1376)

The Jolly Roger, with a pirate ship theme, opened in 1952 and was the first hotel at the beach to feature air conditioning. (P2371)

The Wynholm Hotel was in operation from 1942 to 1975. Today the site is part of the Sheraton Yankee Trader Hotel complex. (P2394)

The Lago Mar is consistently rated the "Best Hotel in Fort Lauderdale" (*Zagat Survey*). It has been owned and operated by the Banks family for three generations.
(P1672)

The distinctive Pier 66 Hotel tower addition, with a revolving rooftop lounge, was opened in 1965. In 1994 the hotel was purchased and became the first Hyatt on the East Coast.
(P1690)

Air View of Beach Front, Fort Lauderdale, Florida F6

**This circa 1937-1942 view of the beach shows the Lauderdale Beach Hotel
surrounded by smaller hotels and apartment buildings.** (P1291)

Southward Hotel at Birch Estate, Fort Lauderdale, Florida

F-124

The Southward Hotel was located at the north end of the beach "strip." (P2400)

A. W. Erkins built the Tower Apartments in 1925. It was the largest apartment building in Broward County until after World War II.
(P2383)

LOBBY

TROPICAL PATIO

TOWERS APARTMENTS

FORT LAUDERDALE FLORIDA

The Southwinds Hotel Court was located at 1630 South Federal Highway near 17th Avenue.
(P2589)

The Southwinds Hotel Court   Fort Lauderdale, Florida

DRESDEN APARTMENTS ON NEW RIVER, FORT LAUDERDALE, FLORIDA.

The Dresden Apartments opened in 1918 at 220 Southeast River Drive. (P2030)

TROPICAL MANOR
FORT LAUDERDALE, FLORIDA

At the Tropical Manor, Carl and Ede tell their friends: "This place has everything you would want." (P2398)

F. L. 106   LAUDERDALE ARMS APARTMENTS, FORT LAUDERDALE, FLA.

3A-H855

A 1930s view showing the Francis Abreu designed Lauderdale Arms Apartments. (P392)

The Bermudian,
315 North Birch Rd.,
Ft. Lauderdale, Florida

Located on the Intracoastal Waterway, the Bermudian is one of the intimate apartment/hotel complexes that can still be found in the beach area. (P2397)

In the 1950s many small apartment-hotels opened up at the beach. The Capri Apartments (P2203) at 420 North Birch Road and the Tarrymore (P2202) on Terramar Street are two examples.

(P2203)

(P2202)

Landmarks

The 1928 Broward County Court House was built on the south bank of the New River. Portions of this building still exist within the current courthouse and jail. (P314)

Broward County Court House

City Hall, Fort Lauderdale, Florida

The third permanent City Hall was built at 301 North Andrews Avenue and used from 1948 to 1968. (P2520)

FORT LAUDERDALE CITY HALL

Shown is a John DeGroot mural at the Radio Club nightclub, a popular bar in the 1940s. (P2813)

A Spring Break icon, the Elbo Room bar opened in 1938 and was featured in the film "Where The Boys Are." The current building was built in 1954. (P1323)

CLUB BROWNIE'S BAR & PACKAGE STORE — Ft. Lauderdale's Oldest Bar — Since 1935

In 1935 Brownie Robertson bought the Trianon Ballroom and later renamed it Club Brownie. Today, Brownie's Bar is Fort Lauderdale's oldest saloon. (P1325)

Chicago native Frank Croissant developed the Croissant Park neighborhood in the 1920s. This building was the sales office. (P517)

The year 1965 saw the opening of Ocean Wtorld, a marine park that featured a dolphin show. It closed in 1994. (P1613)

The War Memorial Auditorium opened in Holiday Park in 1950. Dedicated to veterans, it hosts all kinds of events. (P2268)

Located at 701 Bayshore Drive, the Manhattan Towers apartment building is a great example of Mid-Century Modern design. (P2360)

Started in 1939 in the renovated Granada Apartment Building, Broward General Hospital is located on South Andrews Avenue near 17th Street. (P322)

Conclusion:

New Memories in the Making

The postcards depicted in this book are but a small sampling of Fort Lauderdale postcards made through the years. They also represent a small percentage (~10%) of the postcard collection located at the Fort Lauderdale Historical Society.

As you have seen throughout this book, postcards depict important people and places as well as common, everyday sights. Postcards offer a glimpse into the history of a place and are a good documentary source to witness change.

I invite you, on your next trip to Fort Lauderdale, to seek out some of the sights in this book and to stop by the Fort Lauderdale Historical Society to learn more about the history of Fort Lauderdale. Copies of these images and the other 250,000 images in their collection are available at the Historical Society.

Above: Originally named for local aviator Merle Fogg, and later the site of Naval Air Station (NAS) Fort Lauderdale, the Fort Lauderdale-Hollywood International Airport is the twenty-third busiest and fastest-growing airport in the United States. This is a 1959 artist's conception of the new passenger terminal building. (P1185)

Bibliography

Burghard, August and Philip J. Weidling. *Checkered Sunshine*. Gainesville, Florida: University of Florida Press, 1966.

Gillis, Susan. *Fort Lauderdale in Vintage Postcards*. Charleston, South Carolina: Arcadia Publishing, 2004.

Fort Lauderdale: The Venice of America. Charleston, South Carolina: Arcadia Publishing, 2004.

Gillis, Susan and Daniel T. Hobby. *Images of America: Fort Lauderdale*. Charleston, South Carolina: Arcadia Publishing, 1999.

History Files. Miscellaneous sources. Fort Lauderdale Historical Society.

McIver, Stuart. *Fort Lauderdale and Broward County: An Illustrated History*. Woodland Hills, California: Windsor Publications, 1983.

Index

In 1921 President-elect Warren Harding (second from the left) is onboard Commodore Brook's sailboat Klyo. (Detail, P319)